$\mathcal{D}$EVIZES
IN OLD PHOTOGRAPHS

Best wishes

Dave

DEVIZES
IN OLD PHOTOGRAPHS

David Buxton

Frontispiece: Two boys out on errands stop to look at a selection of photographs of Wiltshire displayed in a case outside Clarke's shop in the Market Place in Devizes in 1897. Several well known Wiltshire sights are among the photographs on display.

First published 2008

Lansdowne Publishing
2, Lansdowne Terrace
Devizes
Wiltshire
SN10 1NX

British Library Cataloguing in Publication Data.
A catalogue record for this book is available from the British Library.

ISBN 978 0 9509099 7 4

Printed in Great Britain by CPI Antony Rowe, Chippenham, Wiltshire

Contents

Acknowledgements

I thank the following people for their help during the preparation of this book, for kind loan of photographs and the fascinating information that usually came with them:

Shirley and Chris Bush, Devizes Town Council, Richard Evans, Michael Gray, Graham Hancock, Becky Jaggs, Colin Kearley, Adrian Mills, Rachel Multon, English Heritage (National Monuments Record), Alison Nicholls, Mark Rutter, Anne and Graham Shaw, Bill and Eileen Underwood, Sylvia Wilkins.

Other local books by this author:
A Devizes Camera, David Buxton and John Girvan, Devizes Books Press
1983
A Devizes Camera II, David Buxton and John Girvan, Devizes Books Press
1986
Around Devizes in Old Photographs, David Buxton, Alan Sutton Publishing
1990
Wiltshire of 100 years ago, David Buxton, Alan Sutton Publishing 1991
Devizes Voices, David Buxton, Chalford Publishing 1996

Introduction

This book of old photographs of Devizes follows quite a long line of other books of this kind that have appeared at intervals over the last twenty years. I make no apology for producing another one as they are, I believe, still very popular and satisfy a need in most of us for an occasional nostalgic trip into the past. There's something comforting about these nostalgic journeys but there's value too in preserving old images for a more serious historical purpose. It's good to be reminded of how we were and how things looked when we were younger, but there's a mine of information for social and architectural historians in these pictures too. Even in a town like Devizes where most buildings have survived without much structural change for centuries, there have been changes in use and sometimes these are quite amazing to see. People don't change much but their clothes do! Fashions in dress change all the time, so one can often date quite precisely a photograph from the type of hats worn, the hairstyle or the length of a coat. We can enjoy and learn from these aspects of old photographs too.

The wide range of images offered in this new selection includes examples from some of the earliest ones taken in the town, right up to quite recent years and with a fair spread across the century in between. More photographs from recent decades have been included than has been customary in previous collections, so there are a number that are well within the memory of readers. It's a fact that we quickly forget or fail to notice many of the changes that go on around us, so there may be a few sharp reminders here! For a quick test, what shop preceded Haine and Smith's in the Brittox, what was the old post office like before its services moved into Sainsbury's and what was in the area we now call Old Swan Yard? If you have forgotten, you will find the answers here!

David Buxton
September 2008

Market day in Devizes, *c.* 1886. Carrier's carts are waiting to collect market produce and take villagers home, farm machinery is for sale, hay is stacked high on wagons, smoke wafts across the site and there's lots of rural bustle. It could be an illustration for a Thomas Hardy novel.

Chapter 1

Streets and Buildings

A very early photograph of the Bear and Corn Exchange taken between 1860 and 1870. The Corn Exchange was built in 1857 replacing the assembly rooms that previously stood here. The building was preserved and reassembled to the rear of the Bear where it remains today as the hotel ballroom.

Maryport Street in around 1910. The large furniture depository of Neate & Sons dominated the street then, just as Tesco's supermarket which replaced it in the 1960s does today. Neates also owned a showroom in the Market Place that in the late 1930s became Strong's restaurant and bakery and is now a coffee shop. The large building visible at the end of the street is that of Stratton Sons & Mead.

The top end of The Brittox in the early 1930s. J.R. Sawyer sold leather goods and made all kinds of things out of leather to order as well. Someone remembers his father having a new leather folding top made for his touring car and getting it fitted while parked outside the shop.

Stratton Sons & Mead were wholesale grocers and this was their head office in Monday Market Street. They had a small retail shop in the building but most of the company's trade was wholesale and a fleet of travelling salesmen collected orders from towns and villages over a wide area. The building is seen here decorated for the coronation of George VI in 1937. The floral display was arranged on the pavement by gardeners from Lord Roundway's estate. The building was demolished in the 1960s and replaced by the present flats and shops.

Monday Market Street, looking towards St Mary's church, in 1907. Cattle and sheep are being herded along towards Sheep Street aft
of lorries and cars.

chase at the weekly livestock market and passers-by look as unconcerned as today's shoppers on this corner would be at the passing

Monday Market Street in the 1960s. Buildings on the right as far as the fish and chip shop were demolished in the 1980s after T.H. White's moved out of their old original premises, on the right here and extending down to the corner with Sidmouth Street. The archway on the right once led to Cross Keys court and now forms a passage way between Sainsbury's and the chip shop.

This view from the roof of Handel House looks down onto Monday Market Street and agricultural engineers T.H. White's premises in around 1980. The corner shop was known for years as Wiltshire's corner, from when a picture framing and art shop owned by the family with this name occupied it. The tall building on the right, T.H. White's original business premises, was preserved and incorporated into the supermarket that was built here in1989.

Demolition and clearance of the large site in Monday Market Street previously occupied by T.H. Whites began in 1988. Such a large clearance of old buildings opened up views never before seen. On the left is Chapel Corner home during a large part of the 1980s to a popular cheese shop. The standing fragment on the old site is the only part that was saved and forms part of the supermarket.

A view of Handel House that only existed for a few weeks between the demolition of Wiltshire's corner and work beginning on the new Budgen's supermarket.

The Boys Brigade from the Sheep Street Baptist church parade in the Street in the mid-1950s. A major redevlopment programme took place in the street starting in the late 1950s and into the '60s. Most of the old houses in the street and the many small courts off it were eventually demolished and replaced by the blocks of flats that we see there today.

One business in Sheep Street to lose its premises during the demolition programme was Underwood's hairdressers (visible in previous photograph). While waiting for a new shop to be built the business moved temporarily into this small ex-sweet shop in the street. This photograph taken in 1958 also shows a poster for the Palace cinema advertising forthcoming films which included *The Whole Truth* starring Stewart Grainger.

Part of the redevelopment of Sheep Street in the 1960s including the building of a new library and Labour Exchange (Job Centre). Here in 1963 new building is just beginning after the clearing away of the houses and courts that included Vales Lane and Plank's Place and the corner shop of newsagents E.F. Duck. The old town school in the background was soon to go too and be replaced by a new post office and sorting office.

Sheep Street in October 1958 as the first stage of the redevelopment was completed and a group of spectators gathered to watch the
was local builder Reg Maslen (seventh from left in the group). The remainder of the street awaited its turn for demolition and rebui

ficial opening of the shops and flats. Councillors, builders and new residents make up the group. The contractor for the construction

Opening of the new Sheep Street shops in October 1959. A crowd assembled to see the mayor cut a ribbon to officially open the new building which also contained the first of the new flats for the street. Underwood's hairdressers re-opened in the first shop (still a hairdressers today), Bessie Pinchin's sweet shop and general stores was next, then came Bill Maslen's cobbler's and shoe shop followed by a newcomer to the street, Arthur Dean's seafoods shop, selling wet fish only - no fish and chips.

Mayor Cllr W.F. Alexander cuts the ribbon and declares the new Sheep Street development open in 1959. Others present were, left to right: Cllr Alfie Weston, Bob Paget (engineer), Town Clerk, Mr Hodge.

The demolition and redevelopment of Sheep Street was done in stages. Here demolition on another section of old housing takes place as a new section becomes available for occupation. The back of Lansdowne Grove is visible behind the cleared site.

Severe traffic disruption resulted from this relaying of the road in Maryport Street in the early 1960s. Much was changing in this part of town at the time. Most of the old courts of Sheep Street had recently been demolished and the town school in this view was soon to be replaced by a new post office. Neate's furniture depository on the right, just beyond the Three Crowns, was soon to be replaced by Tesco's.

Anstie's tobacco factory in New Park Street as it appeared in 1943. It was still a working factory at the time producing a wide range of tobacco products. Formerly the cloth factory of John Anstie it was taken over for tobacco production in 1917. With the cessation of tobacco processing in 1961 it was taken over by C.H. Woodward the printers and in the 1990s the building was converted into apartments.

This is the White Hart Commercial Hotel in New Park Street in 1929, one of the lost pubs of Devizes.

The rear of the White Hart in New Park Street, *c*. 1910.

The White Hart as it looked in 1943, now with its railings removed for war salvage. It was demolished in 1961 as part of the New Park Street redevelopments and stood on the north side of the street quite close to the brewery. Its position can be seen on the aerial photograph that follows on the next page. The buildings appear in shadow but it is the eighth building counting back from the white-fronted one on the right of the picture.

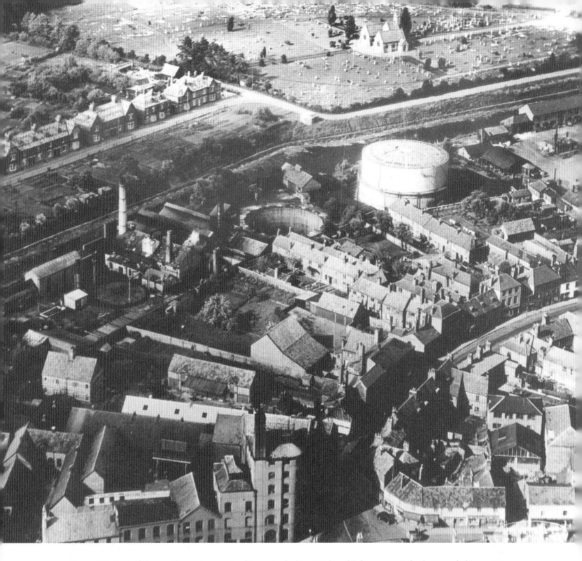

An aerial view of the north western part of town including Wadworh's brewery at the bottom left, over New Park Street to the gas works, canal, wharf, cemetery and Rotherstone, in 1949. Most of the buildings seen flanking New Park Street have now gone. The gasworks ceased production around this time but the gas holders were retained to store gas brought in from elsewhere.

The Regal cinema was Devizes' second picture house, built in 1939 next to the Castle Hotel in Monday Market Street. It is hard now to visualize a cinema at this point which is a busy road taking traffic across town. This photograph was taken in 1956 when the film showing was *Baby Doll,* an x-rated, controversial film in its day.

When the cinema closed in 1959 it was converted into a garage and car showroom (Stringers). The shell of the cinema was retained and a showroom built onto the front but the original shape of the cinema was still clear. The garage closed and was demolished in 1988 to build a link road joining up New Park Street with Commercial Road. This created a through route for traffic, that had until then used Monday Market Street and Sidmouth Street.

The Brittox is Devizes' main shopping thoroughfare and although pedestrianized for approaching thirty years it was a busy traffic street before that. The next few images show it at different times in recent history. This one is from the early 1930s looking down towards the Crown Commercial Hotel at the far end. Sloper's department store is on the right.

The Brittox in the 1950s with parked cars and a range of shops quite different from those of today. The Home & Colonial grocery shop on the left was still using bikes to deliver goods and Curry's shop sold bikes and radios. Robert Kemp the outfitters' sign is visible further down on the left.

Joseph Sloper opened a drapery shop at No 14 The Brittox in 1832. The business grew, especially later under his son Charles, as they acquired adjacent premises, until by 1890 the store occupied the whole area now used by Boots and Woolworths, including first, second, third and basement floors. It became one of the largest drapery and furnishing businesses in the West country. In 1929 the shops underwent a major refronting creating the first floor overhang shape that is still there today. This picture is from around 1900.

Sloper's never managed to acquire this shop, Walker's Stores, which separated the two halves of their business premises (now Shamrock Linen). This delightful view into Walker's around the turn of the last century provides a rare chance to see what a well-stocked grocery store of the period looked like, complete with chairs to sit on while orders were being attended to.

Looking up The Brittox in around 1900. On the left is Strong's bakers and Phoenix Restaurant (renamed after a fire at the premises) followed by Mrs Willis's toy shop, an agency office for servants and Miss Chivers' fruit shop.

Kemp's gents, ladies and school outfitters occupied this position in The Brittox for most of the twentieth century. Robert Kemp started the family business in 1908 taking it over from Evan's outfitters where he had worked as manager until 1907. It remained a traditional shop in many ways, preserving the fittings and features of shops gone by, with glass top counters, banks of drawers for ties, collars and cuff links and chairs to sit on while waiting to be served The shop closed in 1996 soon after this photograph was taken and after some radical rearrangement of the interior reopened as Haine & Smith's opticians.

A section of the north side of The Brittox in 1943. Hiltons' shoe shop was a feature of The Brittox for most of the twentieth century (visible in most old pictures of The Brittox). Despite it being wartime there appears to be a good selection of shoes in the windows.

The bottom end of The Brtittox in the 1960s with branches of two national chain stores that no longer exist.

This view is a little further up The Brittox photographed in the 1960s at around the same time as the one above.

At the top end of The Brittox the first greengrocer to exploit a narrow space between two shops leading to a shop behind was Mortimer's the growers from Bromham. Haine & Smith began life in Devizes in this shop before taking over the old Kemp's shop. This view is from 1988.

In early 2008 The Little Brittox lost a colourful feature when David Erwood retired and his fruit, flowers, vegetables and fish shop closed. The pavement displays of produce adorned this narrow little street for years and closure meant the loss of another traditional shop in the town.

A new post office opened in the mid-1960s as part of the re-development of Sheep Street and Maryport Street corner. It has now been replaced by a post office counter incorporated into the Sainsbury's supermarket opposite but the sorting office remains in this building.

The Wiltshire Friendly Society building at the end of High Street in 1943. Notice the little garden that now occupies the space in front of the tree has yet to be made and so the seats are actually on the road. There is little to indicate that this is wartime except a sign on the lamp post on the right. It is just possible to see that it indicates the location of an air-raid shelter nearby.

The first commercial photographer to operate in Devizes was Samuel Marshman who first advertised his services in the local press in 1858. His studio was at No. 3 High Street and he traded there until 1873. The High Street premises were then used in turn by at least six further photographic businesses (Wm Honey, Stone & Wilkinson, H.J. Wilkinson, Gilbert & Co, Whitfield Cosser and H. Edmonds) up to 1923. This picture taken at the rear of the High Street studios was used by Stone and Wilkinson (1892-4) to illustrate a card advertising their services.

This is the rear of No. 12 High Street as it was in 1965. After some ingenious redevelopment it is better known today as Old Swan Yard, a popular shopping court with a café and specialist shops.

This is Long Street looking towards the town centre from the corner by Hillworth Road. The flags are out to celebrate the golden jubilee of Queen Victoria in 1887.

Hampton's Farm Dairy in Long Street opposite St Andrews church around the turn of the twentieth century. You could have your milk delivered and dispensed into a container at your door or you could collect it from the dairy in your own jug or milk can for a discount price. They also sold butter, cream and honey from the shop. Milk cans, with a fitted lid and loop handle, were often personalised with the family name.

Beale's of Bath, the St John's Street shop that supplied women's fashions for sixty years, closed in January 2004. The original business was founded by Victor Beale in Bath using compensation money he was awarded after being invalided out of the army in 1918. Three generations of the family ran the business and one of the founder's granddaughters was the manageress when it closed. After a long period of restoration and conversion this very old building re-opened as a new pub, The Silk Mercer, in September 2008.

An early photograph of St John's church with a group of boys standing in the churchyard. Judging by the dress of the boys the photograph could have been taken in the 1870s.

Albion Place in Sidmouth Street is nowadays a public square with trees and a new piece of sculpture. The buildings around it are all business premises. In 1943 when this photograph was taken they were private houses and the space before them gardens. Still earlier pictures of Albion Place show neat railings enclosing the gardens.

A brilliant sunny day in Long Street photographed in 1943. The ivy-clad house in the foreground is No. 37. Just visible on some of the windows is criss-crossed white tape, a war-time precaution to reduce injury in a bombing raid.

Victoria House at No. 45 Estcourt Street was built by a Devizes stonemason in the mid-1800s. He took the opportunity to show off his skills with lots of decorative stonework but most remarkably with a sculpture of young Queen Victoria standing in a niche over the door. This photograph was taken in 1955 but the statue has since been removed and the niche closed up. The Queen currently stands on a plinth at the corner of Estcourt Street and Southbroom Road but has suffered several bouts of vandalism and at the time of writing she is headless.

In 1988 as the new link road was being constructed from New Park Street to Gains Lane it became necessary to widen Gains Lane, where it meets the junction with Estcourt Street, to allow for the increased volume of traffic that would follow. Fred Gillett's gents' outfitters shop on the corner fell victim to the plan and was demolished.

Chandler's, or Blue Star garage, in Southbroom Road by The Green in 1955. The Estcourt Street junction can be seen in the background. Originally built as the New Theatre in the early nineteenth century the building had several different uses over its long career on this busy corner.

The Blue Star seen from the other side, facing The Green, also in 1955. The writing on the end wall of the building describes some of the history of its uses: under 'Garage' can be seen 'Repairs, Accessories, Chandler & Sons', the business's owners from the 1930s. Underneath this can also be seen the name of local builder Henry Ash who was apparently also here for a time explaining why such items as drain pipes and chimney tops are advertised.

Quakers Walk, also once known as Keeper's Walk, in the 1880s. This carriageway from town to Roundway House has been a popular path for a stroll for Devizes people for many years. The high banks and hedges seen in this photograph were removed sometime around the turn of the twentieth century.

An extremely neat and tidy looking Quaker's Walk in the early years of the twentieth century. The old banks and hedges have now been removed and a team of employees from Lord Roundway's estate were available to maintain it like this over many years.

Chapter 2
Children

During the Second World War 'Hay Parties' were organised by Mrs Evans for children at Sunnyside Farm near the top of Caen Hill. Horse-drawn haywains took them to the farm for a picnic and games. Members of Rendell, Moore and Ireland families are among those represented on this outing.

This is part of a Devizes school group recorded by photographer Tom Hayward in the 1880s. There were many small schools in Devizes at the time and this one has not been identified but the children themselves, including their clothes and hairstyles, provide an interesting opportunity for comparisons with children today.

A performance on the lawn by children of a school in one of the houses in Long Street on a sunny day in 1907. The show appears to be for the benefit of the parents who are lounging on the grass or sheltering from the sun under parasols. Although there is quite a time difference between the two images on this page there is also a distinct difference in style and one imagines the schools catered for children from two very different backgrounds.

A cookery class for girls in Devizes Secondary School in the Bath Road (now St Peters) in around 1910. The blackboard tells us that on this day they were learning to make flaky pastry.

Some of the children from St Peters School infants class in 1920.

Class Standard 1a at Southbroom Junior School in around 1935.

The 1st Devizes Cub Pack photographed in the Scout Hall in Southbroom Road in 1948. The leaders on the back row, left to right, are: Brian Walters, Mrs Olly Brown, Beryl Townsend and Ron Way. Middle row (standing): Keith Wiltshire, Michael Brown, ? Broadbent, Barry Snooks, -?-. Middle row (seated): John Jones, Ken Surman, Maurice Fennel, Chris Bush, Robin Lloyd. Front: -?-, Eddie Coombs.

Ist Devizes Scouts in the Scout Hall, early 1950s. There are too many people to name but the group includes Ollie Brown, Chris and Richard Bush, Michael Neate, Brian Tilley, Benny and Billy Davis and Kelvin Bishop.

Lord Baden Powell founded the Scout movement in 1908 and a close friend Col. W.K. Steele, of the Wilshire Regiment based in Devizes, started a Scout troop in town in the same year, one of the first to be formed in the country. When years later a Scout Hall was built in Southbroom Road he was invited back to perform the opening ceremony. Here he is returning to his car after the ceremony in 1919.

The massed Devizes and Southbroom Scout troops assembled on The Green for a photograph in 1909. The date is only one year aft

Scout movement was founded and there are approximately 100 scouts in this photograph.

Children visit Father Christmas in his grotto in the basement toyshop department of Charles Sloper's department store in The Brittox in the 1950s.

A little boy looks suspiciously at the photographer from the safety of his front garden at a house in The Nursery. The date is around 1930 and the house appears to be one of a terrace that was demolished before the construction of the Waiblingen Way development.

A football team from Devizes Secondary School in Bath Road for the season 1916/17.

Devizes open-air swimming pool was opened in 1936 in Colston Road off Rotherstone. It provided a much needed resource in the town as previous swimming facilities had consisted of sectioned off portions of the canal. The pool, seen here in the late 1950s, closed when the new leisure centre was built next to Devizes School in the 1980s. The site of the outdoor pool is now part of a housing development.

The little horseman in the Scout uniform is the son of Harry Phillpot, landlord of the Royal Oak in New Park Street. The boys were photographed in the pub's garden in 1921.

A brother and sister portrait study typical of many produced during the early years of the twentieth century. This one was taken by John Chivers in his studio in Sidmouth Street. It was mounted on card with the studio name at the bottom, a format known as a cabinet print.

'Bunty' Butler stands with the family horse and trap outside Leon Burn's, jewellers, in the Market Place in around 1910. The family lived in Bromham.

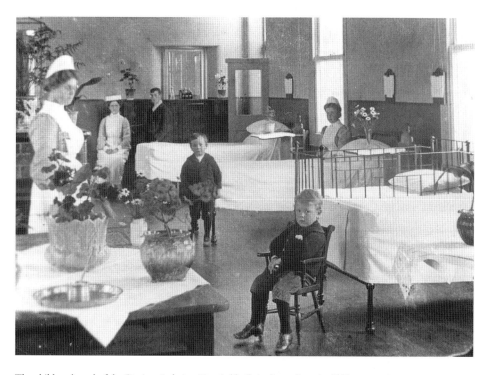

The childrens' ward of the Devizes Isolation Hospital built in Green Lane in 1905.

Devizes Books first opened at No. 30 Monday Market Street in 1981. The owners made use of the courtyard beside the shop to hold childrens' storytelling sessions on Saturday mornings during the summer months. The sessions were popular and attracted dozens of children to hear stories from children's authors and storytellers. Here Roger Day, County Drama Advisor, tells a tall story for some of the regulars in 1984. Devizes Books moved to its current position in Handel House in December 1986.

Chapter 3
Events

Devizes was a garrison town and home of the Wiltshire Regiment for more than a century and consequently there were many military parades in the Market Place over the years. In 1950 the regiment was presented with the Freedom of The Borough and here Mayor Cllr H.S. Knott takes the salute after the ceremony.

Huge numbers of people turned out to see a parade by the returning Volumteer Service Company from the Boer War in April 1901 crowds, like those seen here and elsewhere, for troop homecomings.

e war may not have covered the British in glory but these distant exploits sustained attention at home and always drew large

Reservists march through Devizes to rejoin the Wiltshire Regiment on the declaration of war in August 1914.

The Civilian Training Corps parading in Devizes to meet a visiting recruiting party from the Wiltshire Regiment to sign up in March 1915.

A Canadian Expeditionary Force was billeted in Devizes during the First World War and paraded with vehicles on The Green before setting off for France.

After the Armistice was signed in 1918 at the end of the First World War the 2nd Battalion Wiltshire Regiment was in Dollens in France. This ceremony in the Market Place was held to hand over the Colours to a transfer company leaving for France to rejoin the Regiment in December 1918.

A welcome parade for members of the 1st and 2nd Battalions of the Wiltshire Regiment returning from France after the war in June 1919. The mayor leading the welcome was Mr R.J. Neate.

A Home Guard parade in the Market Place in 1943. Notice the pressman, with camera bag on his shoulder standing in the middle of the road.

The platform party for the Home Guard parade in 1943 seen above were Brig. Gen. Lord Roundway accompanied by Mayor Cllr C.W. Pugh, Chief Constable of Wiltshire, Lieut. Col. Sir Hoël Llewellyn and senior officers of the US Army.

Devizes Auxillary (Voluntary) Fire Service formed for wartime service and seen here in the early 1940s. They are as follows, back row, left to right: Don May, George Canning, Norman ?, Gerry Ruddle, -?-, Bob Gale(?). Front row: Jack Webb, Ernest Rendell (Chief), Fred Chivers (Chair), Frank Rendell (Asst. Chief), Percy Whale. Their fire station was based at the Bacon Factory in Bath Road, which was converted into business units in the 1990s.

This makeshift fire engine was used by the auxillary fire service in the 1940s. An Austin 6 was used to carry the ladders and tow the pump and equipment to fires. Mr H.W. Burt, a teacher at the Grammar School and a noted handyman was responsible for setting up the fire-fighting equipment. He stands in this photograph with Norman Evans.

A parade of US soldiers and tanks in the Market Place to inaugurate 'Salute the Soldier Week' in June 1944 before Gen. Sir William Bartholomew, the Mayor Cllr G.W. Austin, the Corporation and officers of US Army.

This parade was to mark the Coronation of King George V in June 1911. Troops and a band from the Wiltshire Regiment marched past the platform bearing the mayor Mr R.H. Caird and the Corporation. Boy scouts were being used to marshall the crowds, right foreground.

An unusual event took place to commemorate Queen Victoria's Diamond Jubilee in 1897. Blacksmiths struck a salute on upturned
If this is what they were doing there seem to be few safety precautions in place!

ils which it is thought was done by placing a small explosive charge in the base of the anvils which was then struck with a hammer.

Part of the Devizes celebrations for Queen Victoria's Golden Jubilee in 1887. There were massive celebrations throughout the land for her jubilees.

In 1893 the Prince of Wales visited Devizes to mark the centenary of the Royal Wiltshire Yeomanry. His visit prompted some large scale preparations including a series of elaborate wooden arches constructed at main entry points into town. This one was built in Northgate Street. Northgate House is on the right and a view of the White Lion pub is visible on the left. Other arches were built in St Johns Street and in London Road by St James church.

This is part of the crowd of spectators that gathered to see the Prince of Wales on 24th May 1893. These people were standing in Northgate Street new the Assisze Courts.

Royal visits to small towns like Devizes don't happen often so the town made the most of this one. Massive crowds assemble in the Market Place to see the Prince's arrival outside the Bear Hotel and a band waits in front of the Corn Exchange. Flags and bunting flutter everywhere.

Here's the Prince on Roundway Down reviewing the Yeomanry troops on their centenary. With him is the Marquess of Bath, Honorary Colonel of the Regiment and Lord Lieutenant of Wiltshire.

Another scene outside the Bear Hotel on the occasion of the Prince of Wales' visit to Devizes. The party in the foreground are representatives of the Borough Council, including the officers and mace bearers.

Lord Roundway's carriage outside Roundway House prepared for the use of the Prince of Wales during his visit to Devizes.

In September 1879 there were celebrations in Devizes for the inauguration of a new fountain in the Market Place. The long awaited unveiling celebrations to all accounts provided a splendid day with a special dinner in the Corn Exchange, sports for children on Lord Roundway's estate and an unusual lighting display on the fountain after dark.

The fountain has from time to time needed attention and the time had again arrived for some work by the beginning of the new century. In 2006 the town council was awarded a grant from HLF for fountain repairs and stone cleaning. Work began and Thomas Sotheron Estcourt's memorial, including his own likeness on the top, began to emerge from the grime, ready for another few decades of surveying the town.

As the repairs were nearing completion a celebration was planned for the re-starting of the fountain. The 'Fountain Festival' had a Victorian theme and music, games and Markets led up to the climax. Businessman Michael Pitcher (centre) grew up in Devizes and contributed generously to the repair fund. When he returned for the party he was also reunited with two old friends from his school days, Mike Miller (left) and John Hancock.

The celebrations began with the opening of an exhibition in the Corn Exchange about the history of the Market Place monuments by Mayor Don Jones. Here, in a suitably festive mood for the occasion, is the mayor getting friendly with the hero of the day, Mr Estcourt!

A popular event on the festival programme was a re-enactment of the Ruth Pierce story by children of St Joseph's school. Here they are waiting to start the show.

When darkness fell the fountain was at last turned on and a laser light show accompanied by Handel's Water Music played across the Market Place! It was a show to match the original celebrations of 1879.

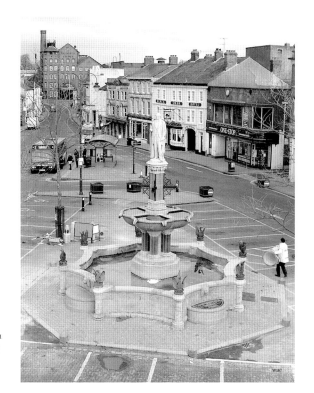

The day after the festival was a day for clearing up and this is a photograph taken from the height of the cherry picker that was being used to take down the festival bunting. An unusual view of the fountain and the northern end of the town.

This is the newly restored fountain photographed just a few weeks after the festival with water flowing and the stonework clean and bright.

On 23rd February 1912 a very special event took place in Devizes. It was a national contest organised by *The Daily Express* to find the best town crier in the land. No less than thirty-eight criers took part including the Devizes crier and mayor's officer for twenty-two years, John Knott.

An avenue between the onlookers was created across the Market Place with a stand for the criers outside the Shambles facing a panel of judges seated in front of The Bear Hotel. This photograph taken by John Chivers of Sidmouth Street from an upstairs window shows the contestents in a line awaiting inspection after giving two cries each.

This is Devizes Town Crier John Knott taking his turn before for the judges. As in other events at the time the Scouts were in charge of crowd control using their poles to hold people back.

The judges sat at tables on the Bear Hotel's steps and the tables below were occupied by reporters from the national press. John Knott came third in the overall championship and was awarded one guinea and a new bell, although traditionally the Devizes crier did not carry one. He was however awarded first prize in the Handsomest Crier class. The overall winner was William Law from Horsham who received £5 and a new bell.

Chapter 4
Carnival

Devizes Carnival first appeared in 1912, to raise money for the local hospital and apart from a few short breaks has continued ever since. Lots of carnivals started up in Britain around that time but unlike Carnivals in other parts of the world that take place in February these were mainly summer, fundraising events. Carnival elsewhere, particularly in Catholic countries, developed out of the tradition for a celebration before the restrictions of Lent, in other words an excuse for a party! (the word *carnivale* means literally 'goodbye to meat' and *mardi gras*, another name for Carnival, means 'fat Tuesday', our Shrove Tuesday). Carnival in Devizes always meant at least a week of activities and these have varied over the years as fashions changed. There have been pancake, go-kart and pram races, fishing, piano-smashing, pie eating, skittles and bathing beauty contests and all types of sporting events. Nowadays Carnival week includes a Picnic in Hillworth Park and an international Street Festival that attracts thousands into Devizes each year. The famous Confetti Battle has survived and the Procession gets bigger each year while many other local ones have died out.

A group of friends dressed as Pierrots for the Devizes Hospital Carnival in 1926. In the group, left to right are: Bob Millard, Alice Millard, Peggy Hancock (top), Frank Giles, Ivy Buchanan, Mabel Giles, Geoff Oliver.

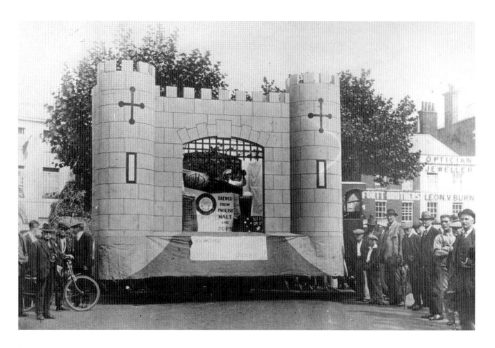

A Wadworth's brewery carnival float parked in the Market Place for a picture in around 1930. 'Brewed from English malt and hops' says the banner. Wadworth's still produce carnival floats every year for today's modern carnival.

HMS *Devizes* was launched for the Carnival of 1925. The float was constructed by the Devizes building firm of W.E. Chivers in the year that their boss Fred Chivers was mayor.

Phyllis Wordley, Devizes' first Carnival Queen, wearing the tiara and gown presented to her for the Carnival Ball in 1933.

An elegant ceremony in a regal setting. This is the crowning of the first Devizes Carnival Queen, Phyllis Wordley, in the castle grounds in 1933. The mayor, mayor's officer, Arthur Dopson, and mace bearers are present to lend some gravitas to this very grand occasion.

This is a typical carnival trade float of the time presented by Stratton Sons & Mead, the retail and wholesale grocers, in the early 1920s. The company's large warehouse in Monday Market Street was on the site now occupied by M&S Simply Food.

This fancy dress group photographed outside the Town Hall in 1936 were ready to take part in the Carnival of that year. Some are dressed as familiar characters from children's stories.

The mayor's car decorated for the 1913 carnival. This was the second carnival in Devizes and according to a local newspaper report an eagerly awaited event. The first one had been a huge success both as a fundraiser for the hospital and as a source of popular entertainment for everyone. It appears too to have been the first time confetti was thrown at a Devizes Carnival. Women carrying baskets of confetti and flower petals handed them to the crowds which were then thrown at the procession. The mayor in that year was Herbert Sainsbury.

A Devizes Carnival float by hardware merchant A.G. Richards seen here in around 1930. The man in the clean white coat is Mr Slade who opened his own hardware business in the Market Place in 1939. His shop appears in another picture earlier in the book.

The delivery van of Walter Rose & Sons, Family Butcher, Sidmouth Street, decorated for the Hospital Carnival of 1926. The butcher on the right is Curly Wiltshire and he is holding a knife sharpening steel in his hand. It was common for trade photographs of this kind to feature the subjects holding the tools of their trade.

Violet Scudamore was Mother Goose in the carnival of 1924. Her father ran a sewing machine shop in the High Street and was an agent for the Singer company. Hence Violet carries a sewing machine in her lap to promote the family firm, as she sits on her beautifully decorated pram outside the shop.

This Carnival entry by Sloper's department store from the 1920s makes a strange claim – perhaps the subject had a topical theme that no longer has any meaning for us.

This group of revellers photographed by Devizes photographer Horace Edmonds in the early 1920s may have been dressed for the carnival, but on the other hand they may instead have been taking part in a pageant or folk event, as there is more than a hint of Morris about them.

Carnival Queen Ann Rogers (now Shaw) awarding cash prizes to winners at the children's carnival event held at the football ground in 1952. Her attendents were Cynthia Bowsher (left) and Miss Sykes. Cllr A. Weston, is on the right (above). Large crowds have gathered for the event and the football stand behind is full of spectators.

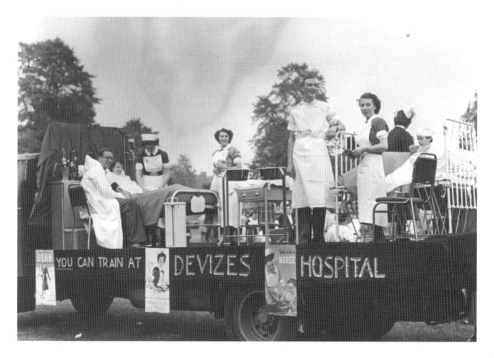

A Devizes Hospital float, carrying real doctors and nurses, entered in the 1955 Carnival. Sadly you can no longer train to be a nurse in Devizes nor even be hospitalised as a patient, because the hospital closed in 2007.

Carnival Queen Ann Rogers with the winning baby at the Carnival Baby Show in 1952.

Devizes Town FC Supporters Club dressed for carnival in 1954. The theme of fishing in the Estcourt fountain followed an incident in the Market Place earlier that year when a joker was found to have put some live fish into the fountain!

Mary Neate winning the carnival pancake race in the Market Place in 1956. She won the race five years on the trot!

Wadworth's lorry decorated for the carnival in 1955. The company was promoting a new brown ale called Middy Brown introduced that year by the brewer John Hawkins. There are two soldiers in uniform on the float reflecting the high profile of the army in Devizes at the time. Hopton and Le Marchant barracks were both active military establishments and soldiers in town were an everyday sight.

Mayor Mrs E.F. Proudman crowns new Carnival Queen Shirley Fruen (now Bush) after the selection ceremony in 1956. The Queen's attendants were Doreen Buckland (left) and Jeniffer Chapman.

Carnival Queen Shirley Fruen with the winning baby at the Carnival Baby Show in 1956. The baby is Teresa Gingell. The lady standing behind them was from the the Red Cross, an organisation that was always in attendance to assist with the judging at these contests. This photograph later appeared in a national magazine.

In 1955 a group of telephonists from the exchange in Castle Lane (known as the 'Hello Girls') dressed up as Ovaltine Girls for the carnival. Here they are in Castle Lane ready to go. At the back on the left is Dorcas Bailey (now Foot) and right at the back in the middle is Margaret Stone.

In 1956 the BBC made a film for television called *Small Town Devizes* and included footage of the carnival. Here they are filming carnival people on The Green. Mayor's Officer and town crier Sid Douse, in his red costume, is also about to get in on the act.

Carnival Queen Patricia Myers and her attendents following the selection event in 1960. Throughout the 1950s and '60s the Carnival Royalty selections were very popular events, always filling the Palace cinema's 750 seats (before it was divided up for Bingo). It was a great honour to be selected and entertainers were hired to amuse the audience while the judges deliberated and the results were awaited.

The Carnival staged bed races around the town in the late 1950s and early '60s. A Round Table team here chases down Maryport Street past the old Labour Exchange in Maryport Chambers which were soon to be demolished and replaced with a new post office and Job Centre. Earlier the building had been part of the Town School; infants used this one and the juniors were round the corner in Sheep Street.

Carnival Dog Shows as part of the week's activities survived until around the turn of the century. This one is in the Corn Exchange in about 1960.

A Carnival parade photographed from an upstairs window in the Market Place in around 1960. The band passing appears to be the army cadet band.

Jennings fairs have been a feature of most post-war Carnivals in Devizes and the rides see one of their busiest times of the year on Carnival night. The association of fairs with Carnival here began in 1955 when Mr Jim Jennings became mayor and took the opportunity to re-introduce the Carnival after it had lapsed for a few years.

Shirley Johnson was Carnival Queen in 1962. For a period in the 1960s the Corn Exchange was used as the venue for the selection ceremony instead of the cinema and over 1,000 people would queue to get a seat.

A Carribean flavour was introduced into the Carnival in 1962. Judging by the looks on some faces the Barbados Allstars steel band may have been a step too far – military-style bands were more common at the time. The photograph was taken by Graham Hancock from his family's upstairs window in The Brittox. Apparently coins were collected from first floor windows at Carnival by people in the parade carrying bags on long sticks.

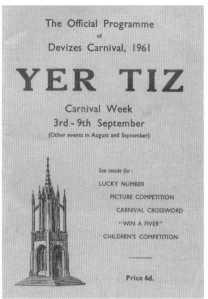

The Official Programme
of
Devizes Carnival, 1961

YER TIZ

Carnival Week
3rd - 9th September
(Other events in August and September)

See inside for :

LUCKY NUMBER

PICTURE COMPETITION

CARNIVAL CROSSWORD

"WIN A FIVER"

CHILDREN'S COMPETITION

Price 6d.

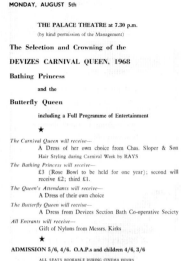

MONDAY, AUGUST 5th

THE PALACE THEATRE at 7.30 p.m.
(by kind permission of the Management)

The Selection and Crowning of the

DEVIZES CARNIVAL QUEEN, 1968

Bathing Princess

and the

Butterfly Queen

including a Full Programme of Entertainment

★

The Carnival Queen will receive—
A Dress of her own choice from Chas. Sloper & Son
Hair Styling during Carnival Week by RAYS

The Bathing Princess will receive—
£3 (Rose Bowl to be held for one year); second will
receive £2; third £1.

The Queen's Attendants will receive—
A Dress of their own choice

The Butterfly Queen will receive—
A Dress from Devizes Section Bath Co-operative Society

All Entrants will receive—
Gift of Nylons from Messrs. Kirks

★

ADMISSION 5/6, 4/6. O.A.P.s and children 4/6, 3/6

ALL SEATS BOOKABLE DURING CINEMA HOURS

4

The Carnival programme cover for 1961.
Programmes were very much simpler in design
than they are today. This one was in a tasteful
shade of brown!

The Carnival Queen and Bathing Princess
programme for 1968 is shown here.
Note the list of prizes for those selected.

Scandal in Devizes! It was headline news in the Swindon *Evening Advertiser* in August 1964 when the new
Carnival Queen Marion Wetton was forced to abdicate after it was learned she was not a resident of Devizes but
lived in faraway Calne! Such was the standing of this contest at the time that she was called to attend a special
meeting at the Town Hall and the Swindon paper delayed producing this edition to report the outcome of the
meeting! She was replaced by her attendant Josephine Bishop (who lived in Devizes) and all was well again in
the carnival world.

The Devizes Young Farmers float in 1962. The missile on the back satired an incident on The Plain during that year when a MOD *Honest John* missile test went wrong and one landed at Fiddington Clay! The man in the middle in a top hat and posing as 'Honest John' the bookie is Richard Evans, now better known as the owner of Weston's tobacconists in Northgate Street.

A popular subject for carnival entries in the 1970s (and often since) was the Smurfs, a tribe of little blue people in white hats who started life as a strip cartoon in Belgium and became stars of TV and film. In 1975 the Devizes Gingerbread group dressed as Smurfs for Carnival. Sitting in the middle is Brian Lyons and standing behind him is his daughter April.

Above Left: The bathing belle competition held at the open air swimming pool was a popular feature of Carnival and the winners had their own float in the parade behind the Carnival Queen. Sylvia Merritt, fourteen years old, won the contest in 1960.

Above Right: Jane and Mark Rutter were Hansel and Gretel in the 1977 Carnival.

Right: Towards the end of the 1990s the Carnival was in difficulties. It had become less appealing, fewer people were taking part or coming forward to run it. Happily, in 1999 a new group of enthusiasts came along and over the next few years gave it a radical revamp. Here Mayor Tim Price, a bike enthusiast, prepares to lead off Carnival 2000 in a three-wheeler, followed by Dessie the castle, a giant mascot introduced to promote the new carnival.

The music changed and grants were found to fund costume and samba workshops and the carnival is one of the best again – a mix of traditional and new styles. This proud holder of a cup in 2001 had attended one of the costume-making workshops that have brought hundreds of new people into the Carnival over the last few years.

Lots of local schools have taken part in courses to learn how run their own carnival workshops with results like this one. This is Kate Copus leading a group of children and parents from Dauntsey's Primary School in West Lavington, with the winning carnival entry for 2007.

Street Festivals became an important part of the Carnival celebrations from around 2000 and they now draw big audiences. The festival takes place on Bank Holiday Monday in Carnival week. Among the performers in 2007 was Kwabana Lindsey who walked across The Brittox on a rope, pausing in the middle to play a jig on his violin.

A band called Smerins Anti-Social club from Bristol were popular entertainers at the Street Festival in August 2008.

This is Portsmouth Batala leading the procession in 2008 after performing at Notting Hill Carnival only three days before.

Chapter 5
Market Place

The Market Place and Lord Sidmouth's Market Cross in around 1870. Before the building of the Corn Exchange farmers propped sacks of wheat for sale, on market days, against the posts and rails around the cross.

The fountain was built in 1879 as a memorial to Thomas Sotheron Estcourt, MP and founder of the Wiltshire Friendly Society. It appears to have had problems with its plumbing for it is rarely seen working in old photographs. This photograph taken in around 1890 is one of many known to have been taken by Mr Clarke who had a shop in the Market Place, just opposite the fountain.

The Market Place parade of shops in around 1885. The building behind the horse and cart houses the post office and a drapery shop, later to be replaced by the red brick Lloyds Bank building we know today. Wilts & Dorset Bank was the first to occupy the new building and in this photograph they trade from the adjacent building that today belongs to Threshers.

The shop on the left was run by Mr Clarke who took photographs of Wiltshire to sell, including this one and the one opposite. The date of the photograph is nicely confirmed by a calendar for sale in the centre window, 1897. This shop became a branch of W.H. Smiths in Edwardian times and continues to be so to this day. Coles, were gunmakers, sports goods suppliers, hairdressers and tobacconists. They also offered hot baths for 6d.

Willis's carriage works occupied the corner position here by Snuff Street for many years. At the beginning of the twentieth century when motor vehicles appeared on the scene Willis's, in common with many other carriage makers, adapted their business to include motor repairs and servicing, until eventually they were doing nothing else and became the Central Garage. The business closed in 1932 and after sitting empty for a few years the Coop bought the building in 1936 (announced on the window in this picture) and rebuilt it as their new store.

In the late 1930s the Coop rebuilt the shop in an Art Deco style (visible in photographs on other pages) which survived into the twenty-first century. Public feeling eventually turned against the deteriorating building and it was demolished in favour of something more appropriate in style. Construction of the replacement was well under way by September 2008.

Market Place shops on a quiet day in 1943. It's Sunday, perhaps, as the shops are closed and the only people around are soldiers. Above the first shop after Anstie's corner, the proprietor George Guy claims 'Here you will find the best, flowers, fruits, seeds, bulbs'. Further along is Strong's Cheesecake Café where the young Leonard Strong managed his father's catering business for the duration of the war and served many military personnel stationed in Devizes at the time. On Anstie's roof is a plane spotters' lookout post and just visible on the right is a reserve water tank for the fire brigade.

The south side of the Market Place in 1943. Lucas, milliner and draper, occupied this corner shop for many years and the right hand corner is still a bank but J.G. Williams the hairdresser has long since gone. The firm of A. Hodge, solicitors, occupied the first floor offices above the bank, moving later to Lansdowne House in Long Street where they remained until the 1990s.

The Corn Exchange in 1943 with US soldiers chatting by a poster seeking volunteers to work for the Red Cross. Many American and Canadian personnel passed through Devizes at this time. A lamp bearing an 'S' on the left side of the building indicates the position of an air raid shelter.

A busy market scene in around 1930. T.H. White's has a range of agricultural machines and a tractor on display and in the centre are rows of poultry cages.

Another busy market scene, this time in the 1950s. Farm machinery is still being displayed on the road side, facing The Bear, and there is poultry for sale in caged rows in the centre.

Four ladies take a rest from market
shopping in one of a series of
photographs commissioned to illustrate
Devizes in the late 1950s.

Market browsing in Devizes in the late 1950s.

Charles Morrison MP for Devizes (1964–1992) stands with one of the winning entries at a fat stock show at Devizes Cattle market in the 1960s.

The south side of the Market Place in 1966. The New Market Tavern has closed and awaits sale by agents Ferris & Culverwell, just next door. Next door on the other side is Slade's hardware shop, recalled by many as an Aladdin's cave of items for sale, goods stacked to the ceiling and hanging from the ceiling. These two premises were eventually demolished in the early 1970s leaving a gap in this row that remained until replacements were built in the mid-1980s. The replacement building blends in well and few would now notice that a new section has been built there.

Strong's Cheesecake Café was so-called after the cheesecakes made and sold there, and at their other restaurant and bakery in The Brittox. Cheesecakes are a traditional Wiltshire item, but the recipe for this one was devised by the Strong family in the early twentieth century. They were made in a puff pastry base and flavoured with nutmeg. When the Strong family retired in the early 1980s the cakes continued to be made by their successors, as seen here in 1988. With further changes of ownership the cheesecakes ceased to be made and are no longer available in Devizes.

Prime Minister Harold Wilson visited Devizes in 1967. He is seen here in the Market Place with his wife Mary, Mayor Robert Somerville and Cllr Brian Tilley (right) who was mayor 1960-61.

Devizes Market Place in 1966. The Ruth Pierce restaurant commemorates the infamous local woman who told a lie and was struck dead and who's story is told on a plaque attached to the Market Cross. Burt's Stores is recalled by many as it survived into the 1980s, a hardware shop of longstanding. In its early days the firm made iron castings for items such as posts and bollards, some of which are still in use around the town. The cross was erected in 1814 with money supplied by Lord Sidmouth, prime minister and MP for Devizes.

A heavy snowfall during a February afternoon in 1985 made life difficult for home going traffic and left the evening Market Place deserted and quiet. Deserted, that is, except for Colin Kearley, the photographer, who went out with his camera and took some photographs.

At around the same time in 1985 the Corn Exchange was having a facelift. In this photograph Ceres gets some attention from a stone conservation expert. In the background work is in progress on the old Burt's Stores to convert it for its new life as a drugstore.

Chapter 6
People at Work and Play

A group of Rendell's staff working on a new house in the Devizes area in around 1910. Rendell's were a significant engineering company throughout the twentieth century specialising in plumbing for sanitary and water supplies, heating and electrical fittings and steam powered pumps. The company survives today within a new partnership grouping called Renelec.

A group of workers for the Devizes' building company W.E. Chivers in around 1905. As tradition had it they all hold a tool of their trade. W.E. Chivers was a major player in construction and transport industries from the 1880s and through most of the twentieth century. The company works occupied the whole of the present Morrisons site; there was a joinery works in Hare and Hounds Street, saw mills in Nursteed road and offices in the old fire station in Estcourt Street, then adjacent to the Bell on the Green.

A group of workers from Devizes builders Henry Ash & Co attending a trade rally with the banner of the Operative Bricklayers Society in around 1910.

The staff of Devizes railway station in its heyday. This seems like a lot of people for a branch-line station, but the work was labour intensive in those days, and it was to all accounts a busy station. The station, which was situated where the car park now is at the bottom of Station Road, opened in 1857 and was finally closed under the Beeching plans in 1966.

One of the London fleet of traction engines owned by W.E. Chivers of Devizes. In the early years of the business they had a large fleet of traction engines with depots, not only in Devizes and London, but also in Sheffield. They were transport contractors to the army in the First World War.

This event in the Corn Exchange may be a trade fair for Devizes businesses, common in most towns in the first half of the twentieth century, but it could also be a fundraising bazaar for Devizes charities and organisations. It is perhaps most probably the latter, as no trade signs are visible above the display stands.

An errand boy stops in Sheep Street for a photograph. Most food shops employed boys with hand carts or bicycles to deliver goods, and the streets must have been full of them! They appear often in old photographs and added to the culture of street life for fifty years. This picture was taken in the late 1930s.

A hay wain comes down from Roundway Hill in the 1920s, a picturesque scene from a bygone age.

Jump Farm farmyard in the 1920s. The farmhouse survives today in Brickley Lane just by the mini-roundabout, before the turn to the housing estate of the same name. The farmyard shown here was exactly where the roundabout is today.

Devizes telephone exchange in 1960 when all calls were still handled by live operators. The exchange building is still in Castle Lane, just off the Market Place, but ceased to be manually operated in 1985. In this picture Postmaster Mr Iles presents a long service award to Miss Griffin and Mary Baker waits to receive hers. The operator on the right is Mrs Bartlett and behind her is Irene Ball who is credited as having taken the last call at the exchange before automation made them all redundant.

This is Rachel Multon working in the telephone exchange in the late 1970s. After leaving the exchange she went to work at Wadworth's brewery as the receptionist and will be known to many as the person who answers the phone!

Staff at the gasworks in New Park Street in around 1910. The gasworks was sited just beyond the brewery by the canal wharf.

Mayor Mrs M.G. Reed leads the Corporation along Monday Market Street and past the Regal cinema as they process to the Town Hall for the opening of a new session of the Borough Council in 1951. Walking in front of her is Reg Maslen (twice mayor) and immediately behind, Leon Burn. The mace bearer on the right is Alfie Rutter and on the extreme left is Mrs Proudman who was mayor 1956-57.

Devizes held regular horse and sheep fairs on The Green. They took place according to long established fair dates, nowadays only marked by the appearance of the fairground. This one here is from the 1930s. The fairs brought many people into town to buy and sell, including farmers, gypsies and travelling people.

A horse dealer on The Green in the 1930s exercises a horse for the benefit of potential buyers. The arrival of horse dealers for the fairs made for some colourful experiences in town to all accounts. Some years things got out of hand and in 1900 parking of caravans on the Green was banned, in an attempt to reduce the disturbances.

The wonderful sight of a turn-of-the-century Jennings' fairground on The Green with all the promise of a good time to be had! There were steam-driven gallopers, swing boats, a tall helter-skelter and fish and chips to be bought from a caravan.

Farm animals were often to be seen on the streets of town when there were livestock markets and sheep fairs. This flock of sheep was being taken down London Road to town in the 1920s. It's difficult to imagine such a thing today!

This a Wiltshire Regiment church parade heading back to the barracks in London Road in 1919 after a service at the garrison church, St James by the Crammer. It was an opportunity for everyone to come out and parade in their Sunday best and for children to run alongside the band.

In 1958 the Devizes Young Conservatives decided to push the boat out and book a celebrity band for a ball in the Corn Exchange. They invited Victor Sylvester of TV fame but it didn't go as well as they had hoped. To cover costs the ticket price had to be high but this made them too expensive for many, and they ended up making a loss! In the picture are, left to right: Richard Evans, Tony Duck, Jennifer Frost, Victor Sylvester, Annette Rendell and Graham Bignall.

In the days when few families had their own transport, charabancs, and later coaches, were popular ways of getting out for the day with a few friends from the office, the factory or the church. The luxury coach still serves that function for many today. This coach, in the 1950s, had parked outside the Castle Hotel in New Park Street to collect its party.

A dance organised by the Junior Gay Nineties club in the Corn Exchange in 1949. In the front row, left to right, are: Ann Trumper, Mary Thompson, Chris Bush, Lorna Bishop, Betty Deakin, Marian Cully.

The Buskers were a group of friends that entertained at lots of events in town during the 1950s and '60s. This is a typical line-up at the Corn Exchange in 1962, probably at a Carnival Week concert. It's not clear who is hidden behind the tuba on the left but the rest are: Ralph Merrett on accordion, Bill Underwood on bass drum, Derek Kimber on trumpet, Eddie May on side drum, Maurice Partridge on saxophone, Razzy Hopkins on clarinet and Pete Lamb on banjo.

In the late 1950s and early '60s Skiffle was a national craze, with Lonnie Donegan the most successful British exponent. Its simple musical requirements gave many would-be musicians the chance to play in a band, often with the simplest of instruments such as washboards, kazoos and a tea-chest bass. Here is a Devizes Skiffle band of the late 1950s playing at the Corn Exchange. Lead guitarist is Alan Fielding and among the dancers are, back row, second from left: Graham Shaw and in the middle section of the front row, the girls are, from the left: Rita Hicks, Ann Rogers, Carol Genever, Janet Alexander.

A particularly hard winter in the mid-1950s provided a skating rink on the canal for the brave and energetic, seen here at the top of the flight of locks from Prison Bridge.

The frozen Crammer provided an opportunity for some motor sport in the mid-1960s. Devizes Motor Club organised a 'Night Rally' when a group of motoring enthusiasts did time trials on the ice. Apparently no-one was hurt and no cars slid into the retaining wall!

The Crammer had also frozen hard enough for some serious skating as Clive Davis (left) and Micky Jones discovered in the winter of 1952. In the background is the Nissen hut on the small Green used by US Red Cross during the war and retained afterwards as a social centre.

A group of volunteers in the early 1950s bringing about some improvements to the Nissen hut on The Green known as the Donut Dugout. It was so-called, according to some, because during the war children cadged donuts from the US personnel, but officially it was the Devizes and District Community Centre. Giving a hand with the painting are Don Neate (in overalls) and Bill Underwood (right).

A music concert in the Donut Dugout in the early 1950s, one of the many social events that took place here in postwar decades. The conductor was Haydon Howells a music teacher at Devizes Grammar School. The centre remained in use until the early 1960s.

Archbishop Michael Ramsey visited Devizes in the mid-1960s and preached at St Johns church. Here he is with, on the left: Joe Fison, Bishop of Salisbury, Canon Con Williams, Mrs Webb. Behind him on the right is Richard Evans and on his left is Miss Carter who sold newspapers for W.H. Smith's in the Market Place.

Devizes Cricket 2nd Eleven team, 1951. In the photograph are, back row, left to right: Reg Neate, -?-, Peter Hunt, Hugh Goater, Dennis Hunt, Michael Neate, Vic Woods (groundsman). Front row: Maurice Hunt, John Leary, Joe (J.S.) Weeks, Cyril Glasset, Clive Adams, Chris Bush.

Part of a large local orchestra about to play a concert at the Corn Exchange in around 1912. The leader is Revd Billy Weekes who was organist at St Peters and chaplain at Devizes prison.

Nurses at Devizes Hospital in the late 1950s help stir the patients' Christmas pudding in the hospital kitchens. Matron takes an interest, as one of them adds a bottle of Guinness to the mix.

In the 1950s and '60s, building firm W.E. Chivers organised an annual produce show for their staff, held in the Corn Exchange, which grew into an open competiton and became a big and popular event.

The chef at The Bear Hotel offering a dish of Devizes Pie in 1988. Not a pie in the usual sense but cooked under a pastry lid which is removed before serving it, sliced cold with pickles. The original recipe uses a whole calf's head, including the brains, so since the advent of BSE it is rarely made nowadays.

Lardy cakes are a Wiltshire speciality but traditional hand-made ones like this are hard to find today. This Bromham baker's shop in the Market Place called Audrey's (between HSBC and the Little Brittox) made wonderfully sticky lardies in the 1980s and '90s. Customers were always offered the tray and encouraged to choose the one they most liked the look of.

A fabulous coach leads a procession to advertise the arrival of the circus in town. A large crowd has turned out to see it and Devizes' town crier John Knott has been encouraged to ride on the box seat and make announcements about the shows to follow. The procession is in Southbroom Road and the Big Top is visible on The Green in the background. The date is around 1910.

A parade of local farm workers walk behind the banner of the National Union of Agricultural Workers in Estcourt Street after a rally in the town in the 1950s.